Sox in a Sizzle

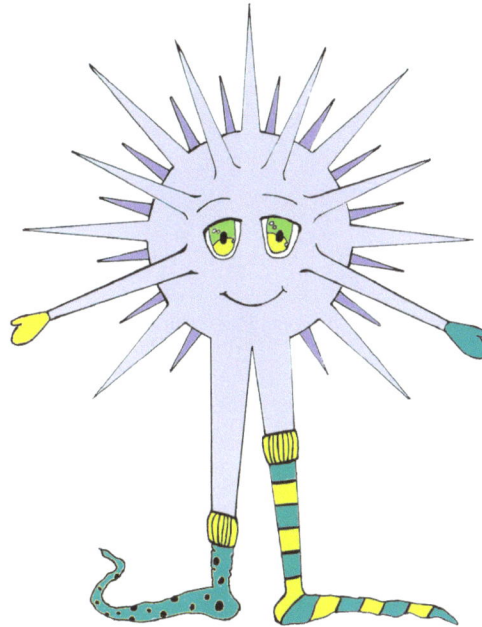

Written and illustrated by
Sara Semple

To Alice and Ciaran

Who continue to inspire me.

Sox went out walking,

Stepping forward, unaware.

That slipping on their saggy sock

Would fling them swiftly in the air!

Flying like a falcon.

Then falling like a fridge.

They stumbled, tumbled downward.

Landing with a flump, flap and flip.

Sox wibbled and wobbled,

On the bouncy, jelly-like ground.

Staring in astonishment,

At this strange new land.

"Well, what a tizzle,"

Says Sox in a Sizzle.

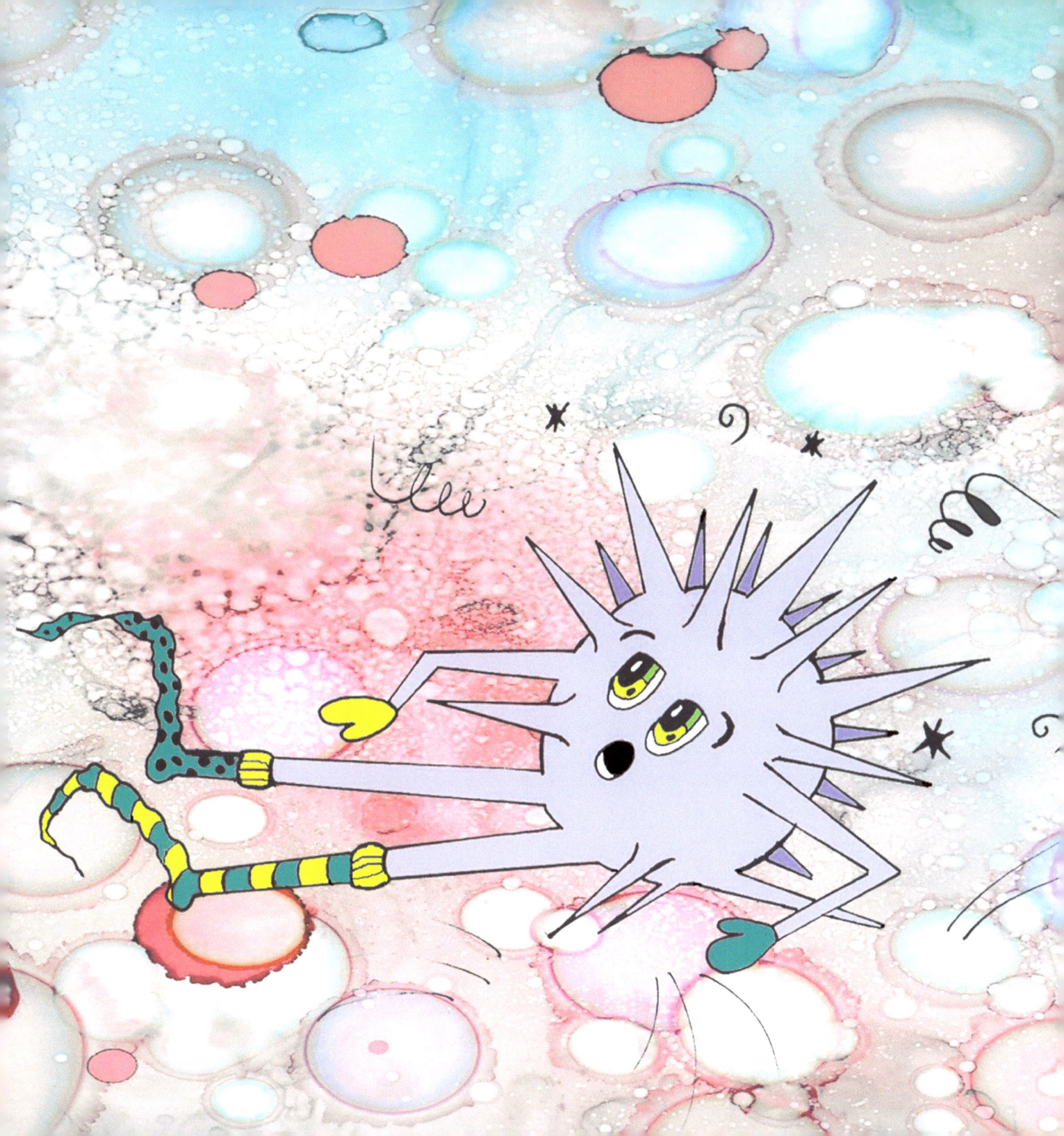

The world started vibrating.

And Sox started shaking.

As a whirling red microbe,

Came hurtling towards them!

Slam, bam, bump, bash!

"Hey, I'm so sorry,

But I had to dash," yells Nova.

"I'm being chased, and in a big hurry!"

"Please lend me a hand to get up."

"My name's Nova, but I'm in a rush."

"I can't lend you a hand, as I don't have enough,"

Sox replied in a flux.

"Oh, what a riddle,"

Says Sox in a Sizzle!

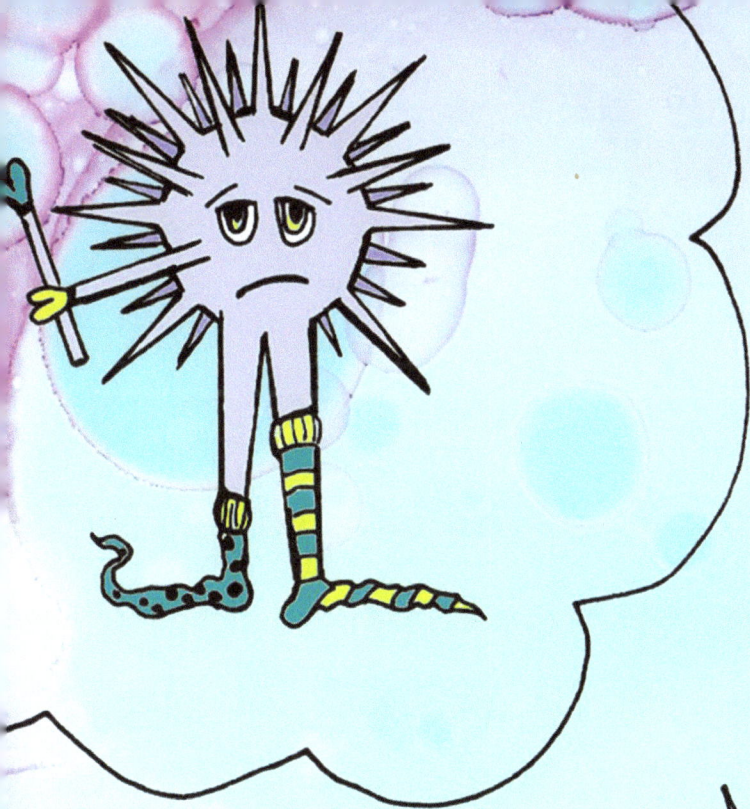

Nova giggled,

His suckers starting to jiggle.

"Ha, ha, you're funny,

But we need to start running!"

"*Get your skates on snappy,*" Nova shrieks.

"*The Bammies are coming,*

And we need to be quick.

Find somewhere to hide, or we'll be in a fix!"

"*Well, this is a pickle,*"

Says Sox in a Sizzle.

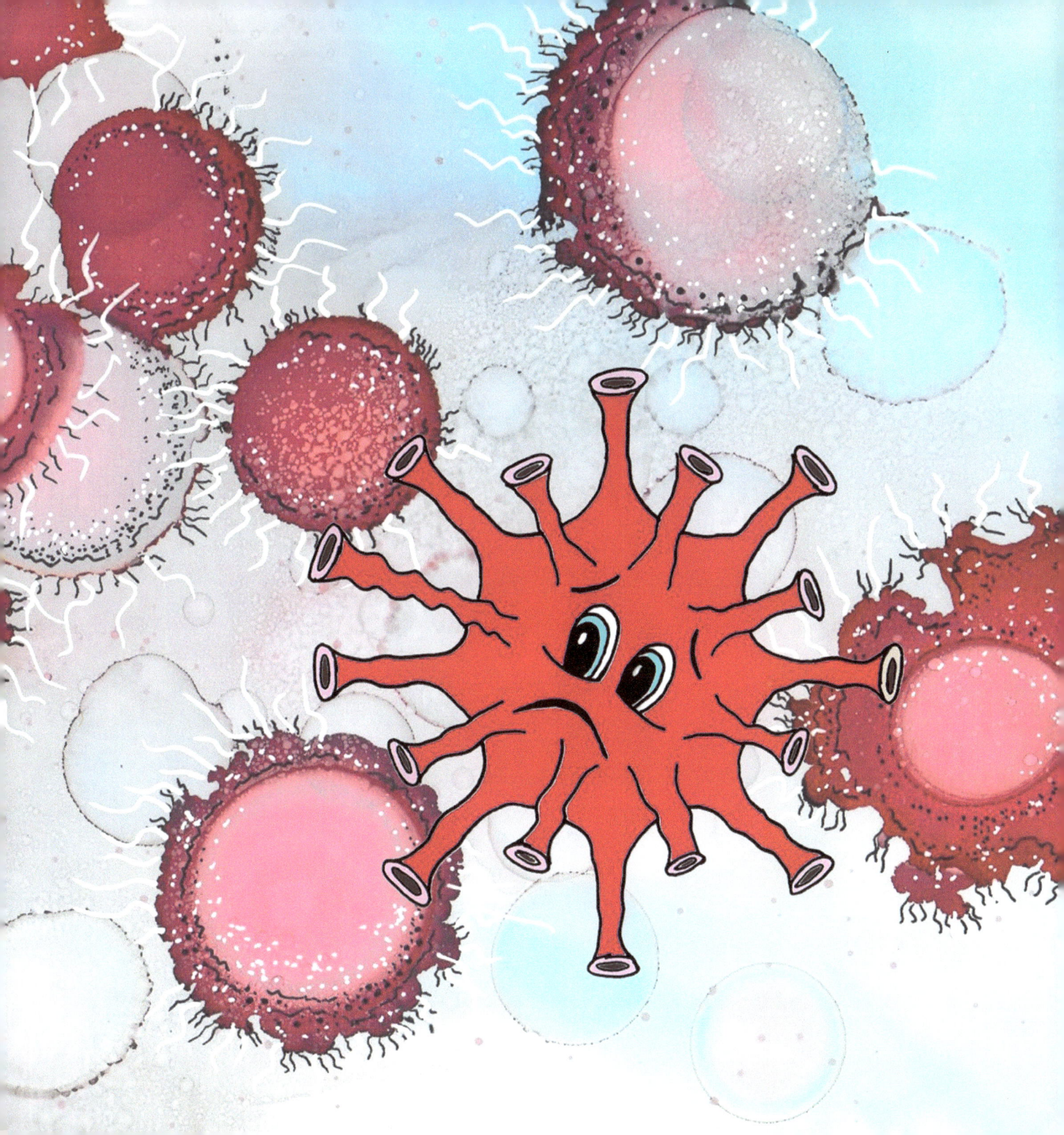

"I have no skates, will socks do?"

Sox calls to Nova, confused.

But looking back in terror at the chasing crew,

Yelps, *"But I'm following you!"*

"Quick over here," came a welcoming call.

They followed the voice and dived into a nook.

Waited quiet and snug,

While the Bammies overtook.

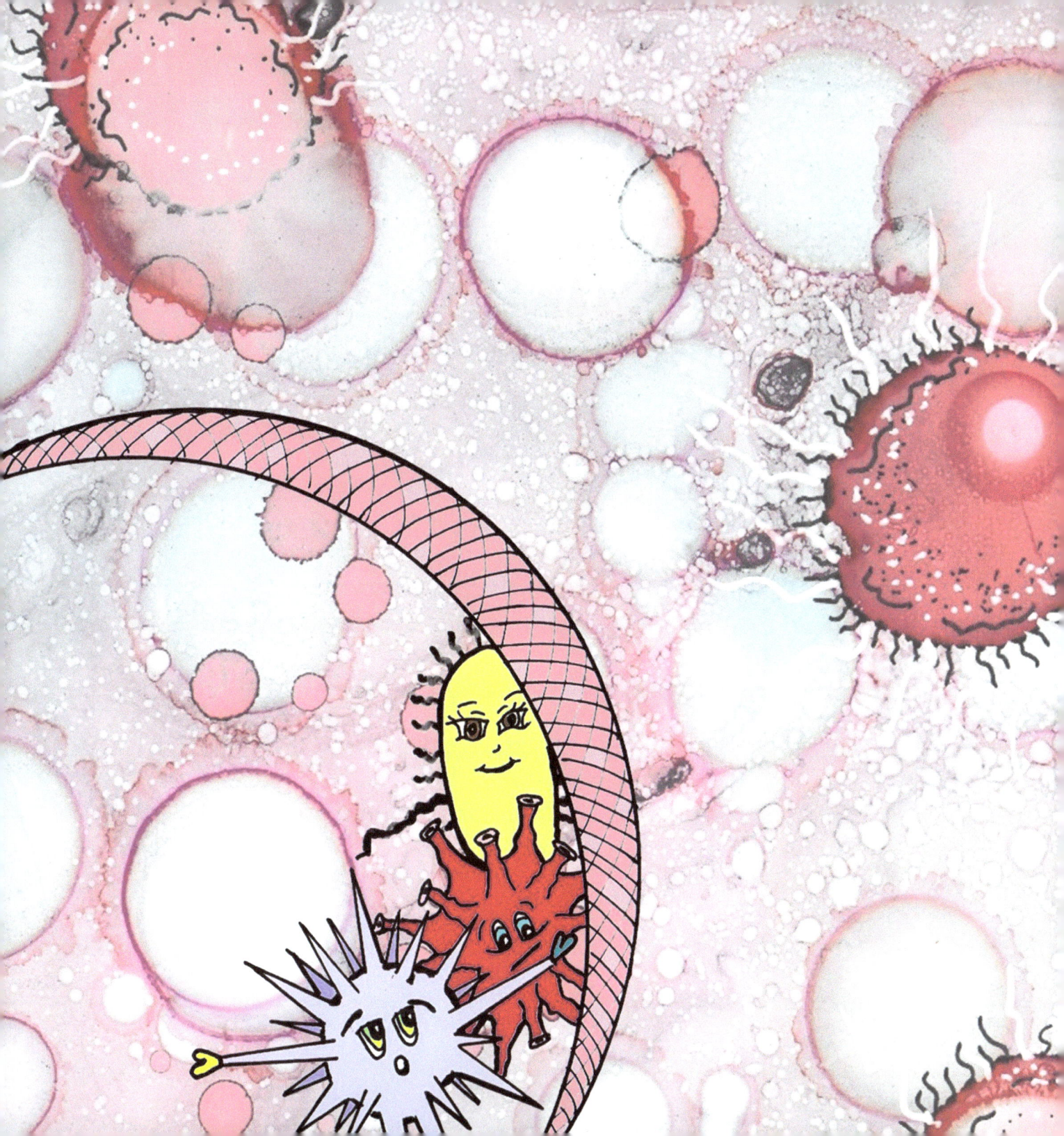

When all grew quiet and calm.

Sox cried out in alarm.

"Oh, what a day, I'm so in a sizzle!

Why is this place such a fuzzle and a puzzle?"

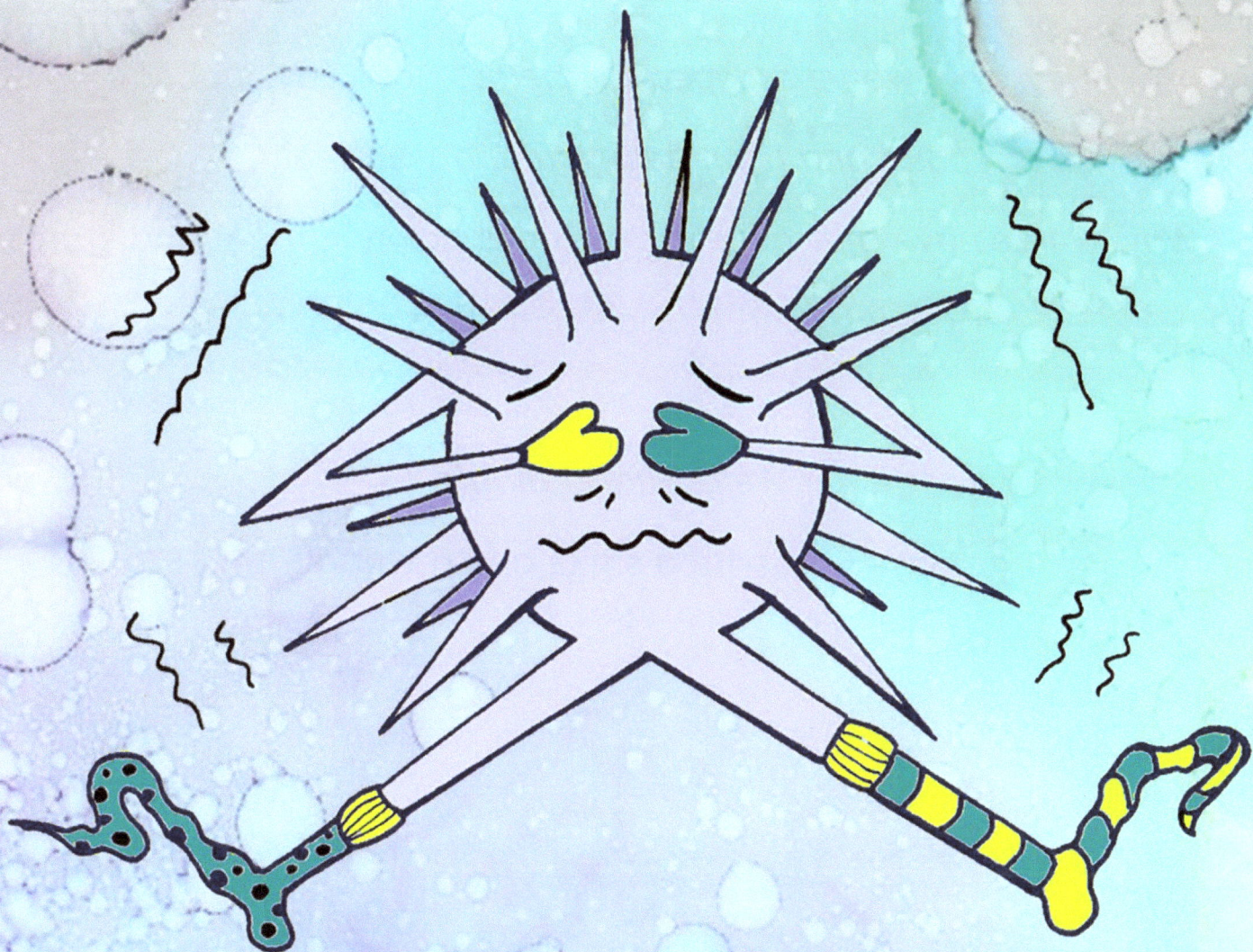

"Hey, now we've escaped the heat," Nova says upbeat.

"Suri and I can help you find your feet."

"Why, where have they gone?" Sox looks down in fright and stares.

Happy to find that his feet are still there.

"Well, what a giggle,"

Says Sox, with a smile and a wriggle.

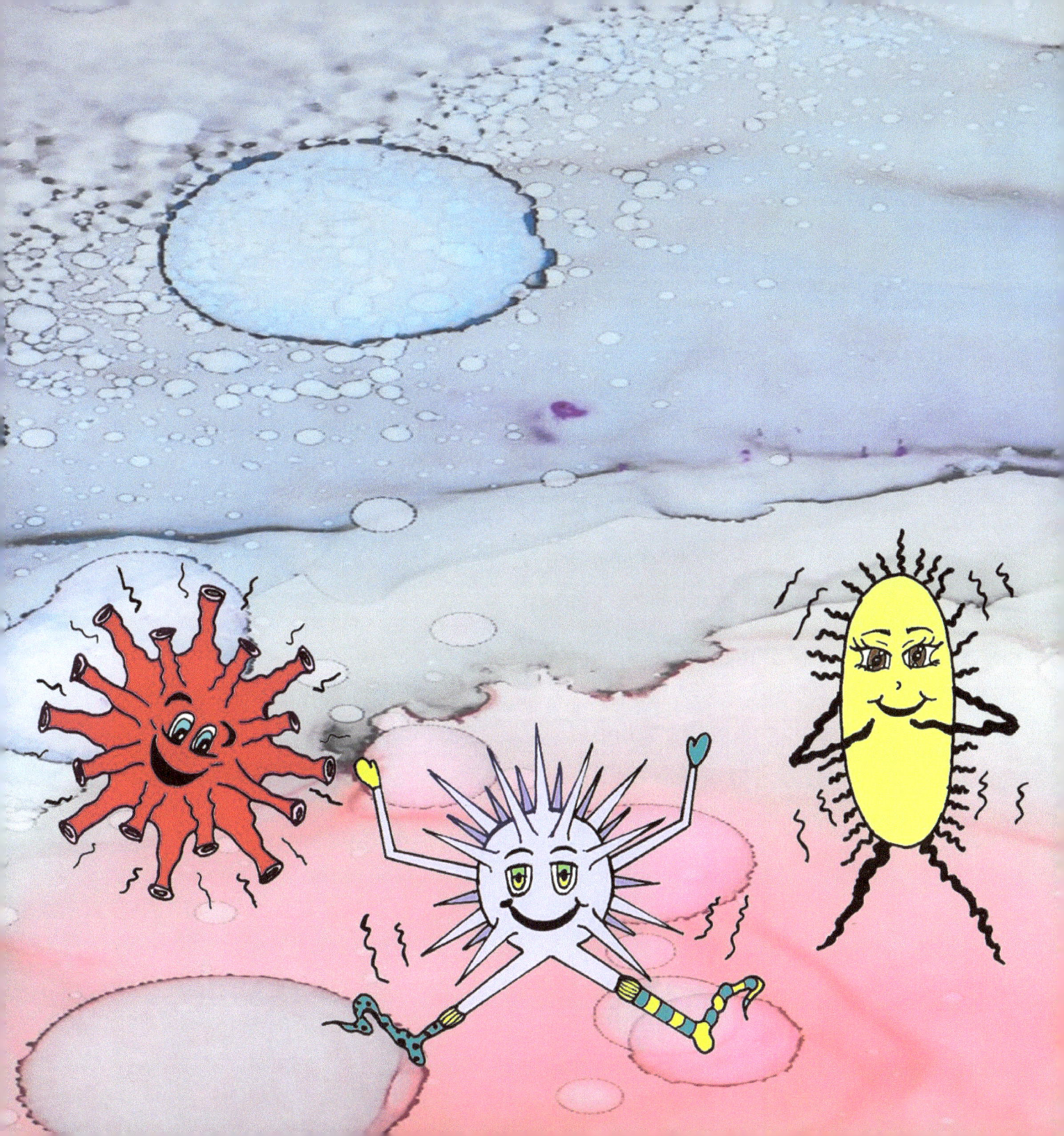

About the Author

Sox in a Sizzle, is the first of what I envision will be a series of books of short, fun, playful stories with neurodivergent characters at its core. I am an autistic creative artist based in North Yorkshire, UK. I was nonspeaking until aged 15 and developed a passion for reading from a young age. Books were both my escape and connection with the world.

My background is in mental health nursing. I then retrained and completed a diploma in Art & Design and a BA Fine Art degree. Leading on to be a freelance artist. I have set up art and wellbeing groups in a broad range of community and hospital settings. As well as delivering support for autistic adults with a late diagnosis.

When not creating, I find much joy in live music, getting out walking in nature, and being inspired to read new authors at my book group.

My son was diagnosed as autistic at age 5. I remember it creating a sense of complete isolation for both of us, at that time. Not being in contact with any other adults or children who understood. We are all different and unique in our own way. I believe it's important to celebrate and accept difference. To be happy with who we are, has a huge impact on our health.

You can connect with me on social media here.

Instagram- sara.semple_luna_leaf_art

Facebook- Sara Semple- Luna Leaf Art

www.ingramcontent.com/pod-product-compliance
Lightning Source LLC
LaVergne TN
LVHW072100070426
835508LV00002B/197